Samuel Miller Hageman

Liberty as Delivered by the Goddess at her Unvieling in the

Harbor of New York

Samuel Miller Hageman

Liberty as Delivered by the Goddess at her Unvieling in the Harbor of New York

ISBN/EAN: 9783744708814

Printed in Europe, USA, Canada, Australia, Japan

Cover: Foto ©ninafisch / pixelio.de

More available books at **www.hansebooks.com**

"The dawn is on the mountain tops."

LIBERTY

The Goddess

AT HER UNVEILING

In the Harbor of New York

OCTOBER 28, 1886

BROOKLYN, N. Y.
Published by the Author, 1248 Bedford Ave.
1886

✠ *The Trade will be supplied from the author's study through the American News Company, New York.* ✠

PRESS OF
THE UNIONIST-GAZETTE ASSOCIATION.

OFFICE OF

AMERICAN COMMITTEE

OF THE

Statue of Liberty.

NEW YORK, NOV 6, 1886.

THE following poem was prepared for the Inaugural Ceremony of the Statue of Liberty, with the expectation that after it had been submitted to the Committee it would, in case of its approval, have been delivered by the author on that occasion.

It is at once to be distinguished from all other poems written for the occasion by the fact that it was the only poem out of all that were offered which came before the Committee for consideration.

It gives me great pleasure to state that the judgment of the Committee, as well as that of my own, regarding the literary merits of the poem, has been most gratifyingly confirmed by three of America's greatest poets in their letters of commendation to the Committee.

It has been a source of the deepest regret that in view of

the severe inclemency of the occasion, the extreme length of the programme in spite of its abbreviation in every possible way, coupled with the length of the poem as finally completed, rendered it necessary at the last moment to omit it from the programme in the face of those more imperative obligations that crowded the ceremony.

The commendable behaviour of the poet under this most trying ordeal has won for him so warmly the respect and regard of his friends that I beg to repeat in connection with this publication the request which I made to the New York *World*, but which unfortunately failed to reach its editor in time, viz: that this poem be printed in connection with the Inaugural Ceremony of the Statue of Liberty, in the Harbor of New York, October 28, 1886, to the end that its historic relation to that great event may be preserved beyond peradventure.

RICHARD BUTLER,
Secretary American Committee.

Preface.

I TAKE off of others all responsibility for any of the sentiments of this poem from which they may dissent and put it solely on myself. I am pure in my purpose, in endeavoring to interpret the idea of Liberty in its genius and integrity for all lands and for all peoples, to bring to it, lest it be belittled in the eyes of men, that breadth of thought and of treatment which seeks not only to trace it in its development from great, inexorable laws of natural growth up through history and humanity to its present stage, but also to perceive the prophetic handwriting which its great Limner-Queen shall throw on the Future in characters of leading light.

I beg to thank most thoroughly the members of the committee for the generous subscriptions which have enabled me to put this print into the hands of my fellow men for the future judgment of mankind, and in thanking them to thank particularly the Secretary of that Committee, with whose noble efforts in its behalf this attempt must ever stand connected.

MILLER HAGEMAN.

Brooklyn, Nov. 8, 1886.

Dedicated
to
Humanity.

Liberty.

THE dawn is on the mountain tops, the night
is flying fast,
The light the world hath waited for so long
hath come at last;

That light whose flattery never fell on summit
or on sea,
That beaconing light, my countrymen, the light of
Liberty.

Deep in the caverns of the dark, doubled in gorgeous
gloom,
Bound hand and foot. lay Liberty, like morn in mid-
night's tomb.

Bursting her fetters she came forth with Freedom's
scroll unfurled.
And in her tireless hand the torch whose light shines
round the world.

9

Lone Goddess of the granite height, with daybreak
  on thy brow,
What royal greeting waits thy grace? whence,
  stranger, camest thou?

Art thou a Persian that thy hand salutes the rising
  sun?
A grave Chaldean signalling the wise stars one by
  one?

Art thou a bright archangel clad in the black robe of
  night,
Who, through thy awful frown of bronze, dost smile
  down on our sight?

Ask of the land beyond the sea toward which thy
  face is set,
The land that saved our liberty, the land of La-
  fayette.

When, for the creed of equal rights, for conscience
  and for thought;
When, for the freedom of her sons, this young Republic fought;

When, through the angry gloom she saw the con-
  quering foe advance,
A light streamed out upon the sky—the oriflamb of
  France.

Our drooping banner caught that gleam when hope
  was almost gone,
While, as it robbed heaven of its first bright
  colors of the dawn,

Red flamed its stripes of morning light, bright
  streaked its silver bars,
And, breaking through the azure blue, shone out the
  morning stars.

It stirred, it thrilled, it curled, it clomb, it waved
  away the night,
And flung o'er Freedom's continent its courier-bird
  of light.

Wafted from off its wings that light across the
  water gleamed,
Till, with twin freedom on its folds, the French tri-
  color streamed.

Behold ! by thy great sculptor's hand, up to the
  altar led,
Bless thou with benediction prayer the worlds thy
  light shall wed.

While trails the red arbutus vine across the winter
  snow,
As if with flowering drops of blood our bleeding
  tracks to show ;

While rolls the sunset-crimsoned Seine into the
  crimsoning sea,
France and Columbia shall stand forever one in
  thee.

Scarce from the narrow bounds of men, scarce
  had'st thou turned thy face,
To steep thy chafing soul in all the amplitude of .
  space ;

Scarce had'st thou breathed the boundless air and
  heard the north wind blow,
And felt the billows break against thy massy base
  below ;

Scarce had the lightning leaping down its spirit to
    thee lent,
Before thy arm was raised to show what all that
    Freedom meant ;

Till, scoffing at the night that came to mock thee
    in the dark,
Thy heart with one electric throb shot out yon
    quivering spark,

The currents of whose truth shall thrill till all the
    sons of earth
Shall feel what Liberty hath cost and what its light is
    worth.

Alive—with all thy memories, with all that thou dost
    mean,
In the great name of Liberty we hail its Limner-
    Queen !

Steal thou, bright maid, the morning's blush, the
    sunset's ruddy glow,
To greet the nations as they come, to bless them
    as they go.

Thou art as one from out the heavens, whom God
  himself hath sent,
To seal forever Slavery's tomb as Freedom's monu-   .
  ment.

Thou art, with thorn-girt crown, that marks man's
  struggle to be free,
A rapt prophetic seer of all thy glory yet to
  be.

Amid the starry march of worlds, peering with
  breathless pause,
On that grand vision beyond sight of thy unfinished
  cause,

How dark thy dawning glory soon shall seem as
  ages gone,
While from far suns across thy face that wave of
  light rolls on.

For well thou know'st, though man hath wrought,
  e're thy long watch was set,
Great things for human liberty, man hath but
  little yet.

Whence sprang the light that lit thy torch?

———— And as
the vision broke,

Pointing the Prophecy of Time, the silent Goddess
spoke :

"Shut up within the darkened soul, there yearned
since Time began

"The light of that immortal truth—the liberty of
man ;

"Through the long, tortuous labyrinth of ignorance
and doubt,

"The slow procession of the Past is winding dimly
out.

"Borne not with outward signs of pomp the warder
heard or saw,

"That light came forth the latent power of universal
law ;

"The light that in an opal holds the rainbow in the
rock,

"That smiles out in its unborn sleep, a cherub in the
block,

15

" Works in the crucible of earth the chemistry of
    change,
" Rends in the nodule of an Alp the ruddy moun-
    tain-range,

" Pushes with gentle violence through seed and leaf
    and spray,
" Drives on with steady doom of growth and blossoms
    into day,

" Opens at morn with noiseless keys the ivory gates
    of night,
" Sets its red sandal on the sky, the cloud, the snow-
    capped height,

" Steps from the stained crag to the palm, the shrub,
    the daisy's cup,
" Stirs the still couch with unseen hand and lights
    Creation up ;

" The light that in the march of mind, from age to
    age, hath wrought
" The bright discoveries that have flashed about the
    forge of thought ;

" That hews the mountains, climbs the heavens, leaps
    oceans at a bound,
" Unveils the future, limns the dead, and speaks with
    out a sound ;

" The light that quickens in the soul, that fires the
    eager face,
" Inspires the hope, kindles the truth that thrills from
    race to race ;

" The light that warms the Golden Page, that tells men
    they are free,
" Gleamed forth on the historic steps of human
    liberty.

" It twinkled out, a lonely Star, upon the heavens of
    old,
" By whose pale ray of prophecy that light was first
    foretold.

" It glimmered on the Orient upon a race of slaves,
" It led them forth as conquerors beyond the clos-
    ing waves.

" It glinted on Phœnicia and at its sail-caught
    smiles
" The shuttles of her ships knit all her sandal-scented
    isles.

" It shed a broken gleam on Greece, and, with its glory
    wreathed,
" She shone with mighty words that burned and mar-
    ble gods that breathed.

" It cast a beam on Italy and, as its scroll un-
    furled,
" A power came forth upon the earth that governed
    all the world.

" It threw a ray on Runnymede from pennon, spear
    and tent,
" And, born of Magna Charta, bred the Briton's Parlia-
    ment.

" It shot a glance on Germany across the Zuyder
    Zee,
" Where stamped with brave Reformer's blood men
    printed—Liberty.

" It flashed upon the knights of Spain and, on the
trampled corse,
" The man on foot, with musket raised, challenged
the man on horse.

" It quickened Russia's frozen heart that long refused to
flow,
" Till with emancipated serfs it beat from out the
snow.

" It dawned upon Columbia and first to freemen
gave
" A liberty her Martyr-Chief proclaimed to every
slave.

" It fired the peasantry of France weighed down with
heavy woes,
" And round a feudal monarchy a free republic
rose.

" In every country of the earth since years were in
their youth,
" The greatest friend to liberty hath been the light of
truth.

" In every nation of the past whose glory hath de
    creased,
" The greatest foe to liberty, the craft of king and
    priest.

" Bred up by grand, heroic deeds, by agonizing
    throes,
" By suffering whose lines have wrought this resolute
    repose :

" Forth with majestic stride from out the dusky files
    of men,
" On whose great like man ne'er hath looked and
    ne'er shall look again :

" Behold ! great Freedom's *first-born* child, historic
    heir of Time,
" Whose crown hath caught those scattered rays of
    every race and clime.

" Behold ! my first bright trophy won—the Bastile's
    flaming key,
" That yet shall open every door to bolted lib-
    erty.

" Freedom, but never for the heart within this bosom
    warm,
" The anarch brood, that darkly dash against it in
    the storm ;

" Blind sea birds, saddening stupidly the island with
    their dead,
" And claiming liberty for that whence all its
    charms were fled.

" Freedom, but not by demagogues, bred up in
    courts of fools ;
" Freedom for men to use their powers by right of
    Nature's rules ;

" The laws that hold the world in leash, the laws that
    set men free,
" For, save through knowledge of her laws, there is no
    liberty.

" Freedom for every living man that stands upon the
    earth,
" For all that be he black or white belongs to him by
    birth.

" Freedom for every man to come and every man to
    go,
" Freedom for every man to reap whatever he can
    sow.

" Freedom from party prejudice, from threat of craft
    or guild,
" Freedom for every man to vote, for every man to
    build ;

" For every man to own himself, to act his manhood
    out,
" " Free to believe or disbelieve and doubly free to
    doubt.

" Freedom from aping forms of cant, that snivels
    drawls and brags,
" From fashions that adorn the dust, but leave the
    soul in rags ;

" From sounding titles strung on names, as coins upon
    a clown ;
" Put up the eagle at the peak, but take the peacock
    down.

" Freedom from all alliances between the Church and
    State.
" That whelm the body politic with sacerdotal weight.

" Freedom from old paternal power, drivel of dotard
    lands,
" Freedom—for power is only safe in all the people's
    hands.

" Freedom for scholar and for school, for pulpit,
    press and speech,
" For creeds that once have ceased to learn have also
    ceased to teach.

" Freedom from ignorance whose god is superstition's
    ghost,
" From dogmas that have made the cross a martyr's
    pillory-post.

" Freedom for man to think before tradition's musty
    shelf,
" Once for the text, twice for the gloss, and three
    times for himself.

" Freedom in all its shining forms, for science and
    for art.
" Freedom for all the industries that multiply the
    mart.

" Freedom from those restrictive laws whose revenues
    have ceased,—
" Freedom—for the best government is that which
    governs least.

" There is a law in things themselves that regulates
    their life.
" That is not quickened or delayed by statute or by
    strife.

" The greater sphere a law doth fill the greater its con-
    trol :
" A little liberty is not so safe as is the whole.

" Where freedom reigns there virtue thrives, there
    truth and justice dwell ;
" Where freedom sinks there wealth decays, there
    gone is glory's spell.

24

" 'Tis from the bottom to the top the social fabric
    dies;
" Go to the ground, there, only there, the hope of
    nations lies.

" O many-fountained mother earth! behold, when
    morn hath pressed
" In iris-winking drops of dew the milk-beads from
    thy breast;

" Behold the fainting myriads on that full bosom
    fall,
" While lapt in sated luxury a few men own it
    all.

" Curs'd be the law that grants away horizoned
    leagues of land,
" That reads God's title to the globe, grasped by a
    dead man's hand ;

" That leaves a scion of the soil in poverty to go
" Without a home above the ground, without a grave
    below.

"Curs'd be that blinding octopus whose phosphores-
cent charms
"Clutch all the shuddering crafts that come within its
spiderous arms ;

"That stares out with its deep red eyes across the
rolling sea,
"And cries, 'Come up, and be ye searched' and
calls that—liberty.
"Cursed be those vast complexities that smuggle fraud
and pelf ;
"Take—take the simple way and go straight to the
thing itself.

"There's not a handicraft that plumes the marts of
foreign powers,
"Worth half so much to us as theirs as 'tis to us as
ours :

"There's not a thing that man can give, a thing that
man can take,
"But leaves him for its interchange more than its
want can make.

"We want the things that others have, we want
 their very best ;
"Break off the chains between all lands, nor leave the
 lack confessed.

"Take off of things the heavy toll, the tariff and the
 tax,
"Those two great burdens that their dupes hug
 blindly to their backs ;

"Take off of men the angry wrongs that cry against
 the land,
"Take—take your thumb off of their throat and take
 them by the hand.

"Honor the proletariat, but spurn the guilty
 wretch,
"Who corners Nature's gifts for what the pinch of want
 will fetch.

"Cursed be the law, aye doubly cursed, that dun-
 geons men for debt,
"That huddles vice behind its bars and frees it viler
 yet;

"That heaps a treasury for spoils, that seats without
    rebuke,
"On thrones of corporative power, a coronetted
    duke;

"The law, high crime at law itself, that says, 'thou
    shalt not kill,'
"Yet licenses two murderers, the brothel and the
    still;

"Feels in its heart the curse of Cain branded upon
    its face,
"That deep, degenerative taint that rots into the
    race;

"Reels, staggers, falls, arrests itself, and handcuffed
    shouts, 'I'm free,'—
"The dignitary of the ditch—the slave of liberty.

"Before the law was written down with parchment or
    with pen,
"Before the law made citizens, the moral law made
    men.

" Law stands for human rights, but when it fails those
    rights to give,
" Then let law die, my brothers, but let human beings
    live.

" Justice ! O Liberty, to whom the people's rights
    belong,
" Justice ! lest be in thine own light thou stand a
    brazen wrong :

" Well have ye made great Themis blind, where Jus-
    tice stands appraised,
" Lest she have horror of her scales if once those eyes
    were raised.

" Light for the women of the world that mould the
    mothered age,
" Light for the eyes pressed down to death with pen-
    ny-weighted wage ;

" Light for the thrones till kings grow blind, light till
    the sceptre falls,
" Light for the serfs, the hinds, the slaves, light
    through the dungeon walls ;

"Light for the lock-step in the mines, the toilers on
    the sea,
"Light for the poor and the oppressed, light for
    humanity ;

"Light—never till this lancing light lays bare each
    human woe,
"Sheathed be its bloodless sword save in the bowels
    of the foe ;

"Light—and as oft, O Liberty, the world shall lift its
    eye,
"To watch, through coming centuries, that light
    against the sky ;

"Let not men see its glory fade upon a ruined
    land,
"On cities sacked by anarchy or swept by blackened
    brand ;

"On broken columns, where the owl mopes by the
    mouldering walls,
"On stony squalors, o'er whose heaps the moony mid-
    night falls ;

" On streets that mock the traveller's step, on squares
whose roar is dumb,
" On hulls that leave no trails of smoke, no harbored
clink or hum.

" O let men rather see that light o'er all this land of
thine,
" On flashing forms of industry, with rays reflected
shine ;

" On glowing forge, on flying wheel, on snort of iron
steed ;
" On ships that pant from port to port with flaming
manes of speed ;

" On human homes of happiness, of virtue and of
health,
" On hills that break with billowy bloom in golden
waves of wealth ;

" On churches, with no sect below, no sect beyond
the sky,
" On love, the Maker's only creed, divinest liberty ;

"On princely charities that walk through the white
wards of pain,
"On broad humanities that bond the common people's reign ;

"On states that know no North, no South, whatever
fate befall,
"One truth, one law, one heart, one flag, one Union
for us all.

"While Truth, in silence from these lips, speaks as if
thunder spoke,
"Looks the whole world full in the face, and strikes
with lightning stroke.

"Ye need no other arsenal, no navies and no
forts,
"No standing armies and no guns to guard your country's ports.

"Here stack your weapons, sheathe your swords;
within the sentried vault,
"Behold! I stand 'mid clashing hosts, to call eternal
halt!

" Defiant as the stormless truth that guards a nation's
    trust :
" Peace is the virtue of a land, and War a palsy-
    ing lust.

" Ye tyrants scoff, ye war-clouds hurl your bright-
    veined bolts about,
" Lit at the altar of its God that light shall not go
    out.

" Go, drape the spangles of the night, go, veil the
    rising dawn,
" Go, quench the sun, the moon, the stars, go, bid
    them all be gone ;

" Go, memory, forget the dead,—still round this
    lighted shrine,
" On Heaven's sublime Olympus set, Oblivion's gods
    shall shine.

" Great Heaven's Olympus, as of old, spread with
    fresh gods again,
" Gods, not of marble or of gold, gods of immortal
    men :

" What gods?—the Lords' anointed, clothed with a
divine decree?
" No!—for at every step they blocked the way to
liberty.

" What gods?—the scholars in their stalls, dishonestly
devout ?
" No—for they scoured the candlestick, but put the
candle out.

" Whence come thy gods, O Liberty, from cloisters,
senates, thrones ?
" Answer, ye racks, ye wheels, ye stakes, ye chains, ye
dungeoned groans.

" Who are these gods? popes? judges? kings? enshrined
with storied bust ?
" Answer, ye waters and ye winds that waft the
martyrs' dust :

" Answer, ye heroes from the flame, ye wild beasts
. from the pit,
" Be they thy gods, O Liberty, by whom that torch was
lit.

" Come from your faggots and your fires, come from
        your hunted caves,
" Come from your ratchets and your racks, come from
        your nameless graves ;

" Come curs'd, come bless'd ; the martyrs' smile con-
        quers the monarch's frown,
" The stake becomes the sceptre and the gallows-cap
        the crown."

    So spake the Goddess and from that grand vision
        beyond sight,
    Came martyr-voices crying out of everlasting
        light :

" Smite, toying heaven's bright thunderbolts above
        thy scathless head,
" Smite war, smite wrong, smite tyranny, smite dragon-
        darkness dead ;

" Watch with eternal vigilance, let no man take thy
        crown ;
" Upon thy deep, colossal calm the centuries look
        down.

" Watch—such a charge as thou dost keep, by all thy
sons on high,
" Brooks not one tremor of the hand, one closing of
the eye.

" By that immortal robe of thine thy form so warmly
wears,
" Welded together with our blood and woven from
our prayers ;

" By every thread, by every fold, by every fila-
ment,
" By every fibre of thy frame through which our life
is sent ;

" By all who suffered for thy sake, by all who died
for thee,
" Hold up that hand for Liberty till all the world is
free.

" And when at length thy lonely task of Prophecy is
done,
" Come up, thou daughter of the dawn, and stand
within the sun."

Slowly the dragon crouched away as snatched from
clutch and jaw,
Loomed that shrived wonder that the Seer on lonely
island saw.

Lo! on transfiguration's height, translated from the
earth,
A queen cried out before the throne in throes of
royal birth :

"Call trumpeters," and lo, they thrilled each strong
triumphant pang ;
"Call seraphims," and lo, with song the vast rotunda
rang ;

"Call worlds," and lo, with rushing pace through archi-
trave and arch,
Came rolling up from cycling orbs the music of
their march ;

While, as the wheeling planet swung through all the
heavens of space,
As He who was the light of men smiled in his
mother's face :

37

Trampling the moon beneath her feet, the pale stars
    one by one,
Behold! in heaven, a woman stood all clothed on
    with the sun:

Still, with apocalyptic hand uplifted to the
    throne ;
Liberty—signalling—lost in light—no light but God
    alone!

www.ingramcontent.com/pod-product-compliance
Lightning Source LLC
Chambersburg PA
CBHW021450090426
42739CB00009B/1702

* 9 7 8 3 7 4 4 7 0 8 8 1 4 *